SCALE High Program

A Goal-Setting Curriculum for High School Students

Created by Dupé Aleru

Copyright © 2017 by Dupé Aleru and Tutors for Tots, Tweens & Teens LLC.

All rights reserved. No part of this program may be reproduced or transmitted in any form, or by any means, electronic, mechanical, photocopying, recording, or otherwise without prior written permission of the author or Tutors for Tots, Tweens & Teens LLC.

Printed in the United States of America

First Edition, 2017

ISBN 978-0-9993214-0-9

Cover Design and Illustrations by Alex M. Smith

www.scalehigh.org

Table of Contents

Overview	4
Getting Started	5-7
Introduction	8-10
Program Standards	11-12
8-Week Lesson Plan Schedule	13
Level 1 School	**14**
Week 1: Meet & Greet and Goal-Setting Questionnaire	15-19
Week 2: School Credit and Attendance	20-25
Week 3: Organization and Time Management	26-31
Level 2 Career	**32**
Week 4: Career Options and Career Search	33-38
Week 5: Application Process and Mock Interview	39-45
Week 6: Paths to College and Financial Aid	46-52
Level 3 Life	**53**
Week 7: School Mirrors the Workplace and Recap	54-59
Week 8: SCALE Board and Exit Survey	60-66
Resources	**67**
Weekly, Monthly, Quarterly Goal Sheets	68-70
College Systems, A-G Requirement, Financial Aid & Grants, and Answer Keys	71-75
Sample Lesson Plan with Definitions	76
Tips for Working with Students	77
Acknowledgements	78
About the Founder and Contact Information	79

Overview

SCALE High's goal-setting curriculum is designed for high school students to reflect, examine, and interpret upon their life experiences, so that they can transform their deepest passions into reality. This reflection process will allow students to become more self-aware and discover how their gifts and talents can be of service to the world. By uncovering their limiting beliefs, students will understand how negative self-talk can hold them back from reaching their full potential. As students engage with the program week-by-week, they will start to commit to a more powerful way of thinking that will manifest positive results in their lives.

This curriculum is meant to act as a step-by-step guide to help you, the educator, coach students on how to create an effective roadmap that clearly states the goals and action steps that they will take in order to achieve success in school, career, and life. Each week you will present a new topic and lesson to your students that will require them to engage in hands-on exercises and discussions. The weekly lessons promote essential life skills that may or may not be taught in school or at home, but will increase a student's understanding of the world and equip them with the necessary tools to live a productive and fulfilling life.

With SCALE High's program, you will help your students learn how to think critically, and build the skills and insight they need to live and thrive in a 21st century world.

Duties and Program Rules

Getting Started

Academic Coach Duties

Duties apply if the program is not administered by a school staff member (e.g., intern).

Requirements
- Submit a valid tuberculosis (TB) health screening certificate
- Conduct and submit proof of a criminal background check
- Provide appropriate paperwork for the internship, provided by your university
- Act as a referring organization under the current memorandum of understanding or contract
- Promote practices that align with those of the district and the State of California (or the appropriate state's) Education Codes
- Maintain full responsibility for your student and the appearance of the building during the hours you are present—leave the space as you found it
- Adhere to the dress code at all times
- Do not show visible tattoos or piercings while on school grounds

Pledge
As a representative of the SCALE High Program, I pledge to…
- Implement lessons and exercises aligned with SCALE High standards that support the academic success of all students
- Maintain and support positive relationships between adults and students
- Promote a sense of safety among my students at the site
- Promote positive leadership among my students
- Respect and honor my students' cultural diversity
- Adapt the program and exercises, when necessary, for English Language Learners (ELL), students with disabilities, gifted students, and students with special needs
- Ensure the health and safety of all my students, at all times
- Follow school safety and emergency procedures
- Communicate and collaborate with teachers or administration to share my students' individual strengths, achievements, or challenges

Expectations & Outcomes
- Coach must model professional behavior at all times
- Coach must protect and appreciate the need for every student's confidentiality
- Coach must stay informed of updates and changes to the program
- Coach must assist students in completing the 8-week program successfully
- Coach must comply with all attendance procedures and regulations

Student Expectations

- Have a positive attitude
- Have a willingness to learn and succeed
- Be open and honest with your Coach
- Be respectful of your Coach at all times
- Use appropriate language during school and program hours
- Leave all electronics in a backpack or purse during the program
- Adhere to school rules, policies, and procedures at all times
- Come to sessions on time and ready to learn
- Bring all necessary materials to the sessions
- Stay organized with the given materials
- Participate in all individual or group exercises
- Listen to your Coach

Program Rules

Come to the sessions prepared

Be respectful

Listen to instructions

No cellphones

No sidebar conversations

Participate in all exercises

Introduction

About SCALE High
SCALE High brings together skilled college students and teachers to mentor high school students in the area of goal-setting. The program empowers the high school students to embrace a positive way of thinking that will inspire them to *scale high* when planning for the future.

Our Mission
It is the mission of SCALE High to provide high school students with the knowledge of how to set SMART goals in every aspect of their lives while mastering the art of taking action. As a result, students will be better equipped to think about the future and be motivated to turn their visions into reality.

What Does SCALE High Stand For?
SCALE stands for School, Career, and Life Enrichment.

Why Set Goals?
People in all walks of life—from athletes to entrepreneurs—set goals in order to be successful. Setting goals will help students choose where they want to go in life. And by knowing exactly what they want to accomplish, students will learn where they have to start.

Expected Student Outcomes
By the end of the 8-week program, each student who has successfully completed the SCALE High curriculum will know and understand how to:
- Set SMART goals
- Be well prepared in all academic disciplines
- Have a higher motivation to succeed in all endeavors they set out to do
- Exhibit a sense of pride and satisfaction in their performance

SCALE High's Tier Levels

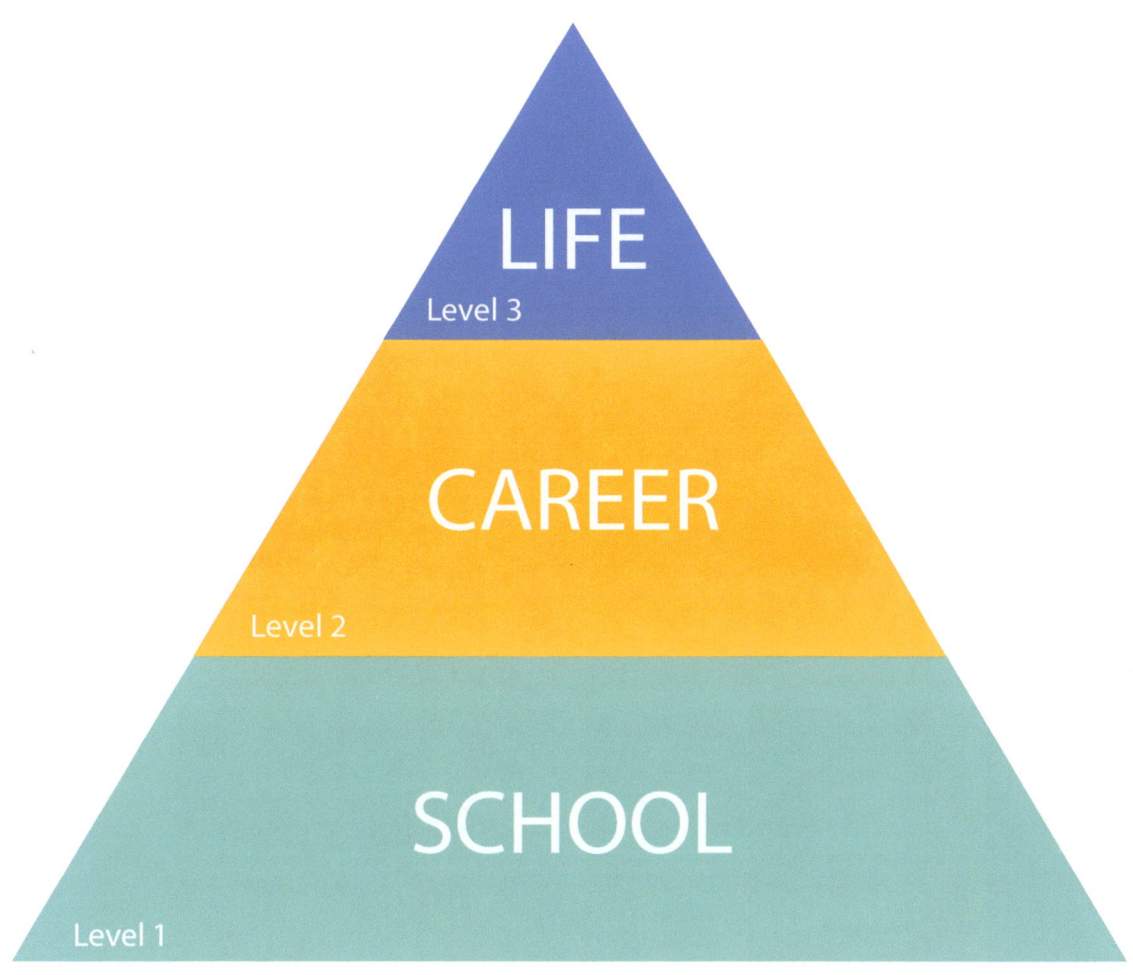

A Breakdown of Each Tier Level

Level 1 – School
Set the foundation for your 1-2 year goals.

Level 2 – Career
Build upon your foundation and work towards your 5-year goals.

Level 3 – Life
Create your big picture plan to serve as a source of inspiration as you work towards achieving your 10-year goals.

Envision Your Future!

SCALE High's goal-setting program encourages students to envision their futures and take action in order to manifest their visions into reality. A SCALE board (or vision board) is used to showcase a student's SMART goals, which they set within SCALE High's tier levels.

SCALE Board

Each week, as students add more goals to each tier, they will be required to cut out pictures that correspond with each goal. The pictures will be placed on their SCALE board during Week 8.

Program Standards for SCALE High Curriculum
Grade 9 Through 12

Notice
Tutors for Tots, Tweens & Teens LLC acknowledge that the standards below have no affiliation or connection to the California Common Core Standards and Content Standards, adopted by the California State Board of Education; meaning, all information below is the sole creation and proprietary information of SCALE High and Tutors for Tots, Tweens & Teens LLC, and is not applicable or related in any way to the California Department of Education's Content Standards, California Common Core Standards, its subsidiaries, or affiliates.

A Message from the Founder
The SCALE High standards were developed to address the importance of goal-setting for students in grades 9-12. Goal-setting, academic success, and overall life success go hand-in-hand. Students who know where they want to go in life will know where they have to start—and in turn, will become more productive members of society. The goal-setting standards define the essential skills and knowledge that high school students should acquire prior to completing high school.

Introduction
The goal-setting standards reflect SCALE High's commitment to school, career, and life enrichment. They serve as a basis for learning how to visualize effectively where one wants to go in life, and how to actively create SMART goals to use as a blueprint for one's future.

Background of Standards
In June 2014, Dupé Aleru founded the SCALE High goal-setting standards to help shape the way students in grades 9-12 plan for their futures. The standards help ensure that students are provided with the vital knowledge, skills, and confidence they need to accomplish anything in life, taught through the use of goal-setting.

Goal-Setting Standards for Your Student

Student will demonstrate the ability to use goal-setting skills to enhance his/her life. The following are the SCALE High Standards for each student in the program. Each Coach should review these standards with his/her student(s).

Each student should:
Standard 1: Brainstorm and answer questions about school, career, and life
Standard 1.1: Distinguish the difference between SCALE High's tier levels (school, career, and life)
Standard 1.2: Begin an initial outline of school, career, and life goals
Standard 1.3: Identify steps to achieve and maintain 1-2 year, 5-year, and 10-year goals
Standard 1.4: Develop a visual representation of these goals
Standard 2: Speak to a counselor or mentor about current school credits, to make sure the student is on the right path to graduation
Standard 2.1: Speak to a counselor or mentor about all graduation requirements, and any plans after high school
Standard 3: Set a short-term goal: maintain great attendance in school
Standard 3.1: Identify and understand how certain aspects of school mirror the workplace and world
Standard 4: List some areas that could use organization in their life (e.g., classes, schedules, etc.) and how he/she plans to get them in order
Standard 5: Make a plan to manage time appropriately during the school week
Standard 6: Find time to learn how to: apply for a job; learn about the interview process; and how to create a resume and cover letter
Standard 6.1: Practice a mock interview with an adult
Standard 7: Demonstrate knowledge about the various college systems: 2-year college, 4-year university, and graduate school
Standard 8: Make a personal commitment to learn about financial aid and grants
Standard 9: Monitor short-term school goals in regards to graduation
Standard 10: Monitor progress towards a life goal

8-Week Lesson Plan

	Lessons and Exercises	SCALE Board
Coaches: Each week, complete two exercises. Follow the order of the bullet points. Meet with your student twice a week for 30-45 minutes.		
Week 1	• Meet & Greet • Intro to SCALE High • Questionnaire • Exercise 1	Ask your student to cut out 3 pictures and keep these in folder for their SCALE board.
Week 2	• School Credit • Exercise 2 • Attendance • Exercise 3	Ask your student to cut out 3 pictures and keep these in folder for their SCALE board.
Week 3	• Organization • Exercise 4 • Time Management • Exercise 5	Ask your student to cut out 3 pictures and keep these in folder for their SCALE board.
Week 4	• Career Options • Exercise 6 • Career Search • Exercise 7	Ask your student to cut out 3 pictures and keep these in folder for their SCALE board.
Week 5	• Application Process • Exercise 8 • Mock Interview • Exercise 9	Ask your student to cut out 3 pictures and keep these in folder for their SCALE board.
Week 6	• Paths to College • Exercise 10 • Financial Aid • Exercise 11	Ask your student to cut out 3 pictures and keep these in folder for their SCALE board.
Week 7	• School Mirrors Work • Exercise 12 • Recap • Exercise 13	Ask your student to cut out 3 pictures and keep these in folder for their SCALE board.
Week 8	• SCALE Board • Exercise 14 • Exit Survey • Exercise 15	Have your student put his/her SCALE board together and share it with you (and any classmates).

Level 1

School

Set the Foundation

1-2 Year Goals

Meet & Greet and Goal-Setting Questionnaire

Week 1

Level 1 - Days 1 & 2	Week 1 of SCALE High Lesson Plan
SCALE Standards for Day 1 & 2	**Standard 1:** Brainstorm and answer questions about school, career, and life **Standard 1.1:** Distinguish the difference between SCALE High's tier levels (school, career, and life) **Standard 1.2:** Begin an initial outline of school, career, and life goals
Anticipatory Set	Day 1: Welcome your student(s) to SCALE High. *Coach Script*: Have you heard of goal-setting? This week we will spend time learning about how to set SMART goals to help you be successful in school and life. Show Week 1 video to your student. Day 2: Administer the goal-setting questionnaire to help your student brainstorm ideas about school, career, and life goals.
Objective	Student will be able to describe his/her passions or talents by completing the goal-setting questionnaire with 80% accuracy.
Essential Question	*Ask your student,* "Why do you think it is important to set goals for all aspects of your life?"
Purpose	To identify your student's passions or talents.
Input	Day 1: Coach explains instructions to student and facilitates the, "Me to a Tee" activity on **page 17**. Coach also summarizes **pages 7-10, 12**. Coach administers **pages 68-70**. Day 2: Coach administers **page 18 (pre-test) and page 19**.
Modeling	Coach will show his/her own "Me to a Tee" activity.
Check for Understanding	**Handprint Exercise:** Ask your student to draw their handprint, and in each finger, write one thing they learned that day.
Guided Practice (5-10 min)	Day 1: Student constructs his/her own "Me to a Tee" activity and shares. Day 2: Student produces goals for "Exercise 1" (School goals only).
Closure (EQ. Answer)	*Coach Script:* By knowing exactly what you want to accomplish, you will know where you need to start.
Independent Practice	Student is to select three pictures (online or from a magazine) to cut and place on a SCALE board for Week 8. Pictures should represent goals within SCALE High's first tier level: School.
Materials	SCALE High teaching manual, magazines, construction paper, copy of the "Goal-Setting Questionnaire," copy of "Exercise 1," and a pencil.

Day 1

Meet & Greet

"Me to a Tee"

Give your student a piece of paper cut out in the shape of a t-shirt. Ask them to place their name on the shirt, and one word that describes them. Then have them design the rest of the shirt with items that represent them. After they are finished, share your t-shirts. *Note: Coaches should have their t-shirts made prior to the session.*

Day 2

Provide this Goal-Setting Questionnaire to your student Week 1 and Week 8.

Goal-Setting Questionnaire

Name: Date:

Student Directions: Read the following questions carefully. Take 10 minutes to answer them as truthfully and completely as possible.

1) What are your passions and talents? List at least three.
   1.
   2.
   3.

2) What do you care about, or what means the most to you?

3) What kind of person are you? (Type of student; son/daughter; sibling; friend, etc.)

4) What are you good at? What are your strengths and weaknesses?

5) What kind of person do you want to become?

6) Are you organized? Do you manage your time wisely?

7) Are you prepared and on track to graduate high school?

8) Do you want to go to college? If so, what type of college and why?

9) What do you want to do for a career? How do you plan on achieving that goal?

10) Where do you see yourself in 10 years? (Family; career goals; etc.)

11) What do you hope to get out of this program? Are you determined to work hard?

Day 2

Exercise 1

Name: Date:

Student Directions: Go over the questionnaire with your Coach and explain why you answered each question the way you did. Then fill out the below flow chart by listing six School goals. Write your answers – as bullet points – in the blue boxes. Be as specific as possible.

Once you have completed this chart, keep it in a safe place, as you will be using it later in the program.

Examples:
School goal – have perfect attendance for the rest of the semester
Career goal – get accepted into a CSU
Life goal – have a family one day

Week 2

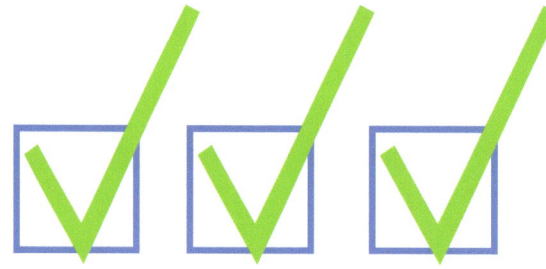

School Credit and Attendance

Level 1 - Days 1 & 2	Week 2 of SCALE High Lesson Plan
SCALE Standards	**Standard 2:** Speak to a counselor or mentor about current school credits, to make sure the student is on the right path to graduation **Standard 2.1:** Speak to a counselor or mentor about all graduation requirements, and any plans after high school **Standard 3:** Set a short-term goal: maintain great attendance in school
Anticipatory Set	Day 1: *Ask your student,* "Do you know how many credits you currently have, and would need to graduate high school? Today you will find out." Show Week 2 video to your student. Day 2: Look over your student's attendance history and discuss the importance of showing up to school every day.
Objective	Student will be able to record their credits (per quarter) by accurately analyzing their school transcripts.
Essential Question	*Ask your student,* "Why do you think it is important to keep a record of your credits?"
Purpose	To help your student identify their current school credits and requirements for graduation.
Input	Day 1: Coach will facilitate **page 70.** Prior to the session, you will gather your student's transcripts and administer **pages 22-23.** Day 2: Prior to the session, you will gather your student's attendance records and administer **pages 24-25.**
Modeling	You will explain how to keep a record of credits.
Check for Understanding	Have your student complete this thought: I need ___ credits to graduate high school.
Guided Practice (5-10 min)	Day 1: Review, with your student, their transcript; and identify credits for each year and subject completed. Day 2: Have your student record weekly attendance for each class (this will continue through Week 8).
Closure (EQ. Answer)	*Coach Script:* By keeping record of your credits, you will know how many you'll need each quarter to graduate high school.
Independent Practice	Student is to select three pictures (online or from a magazine) to cut and place on their SCALE board for Week 8. Pictures should represent goals within SCALE High's first tier level: School.
Materials	SCALE High teaching manual, transcripts, attendance records, copy of "Exercise 2," copy of "Weekly Class Attendance Record" (for each class), magazines, and a pencil.

Day 1

Exercise 2

INPUT

Coach Script: In order to graduate from a California public high school, you must complete state and local graduation requirements. Creating a high school "Credit Planner" during your four years of high school will allow you to keep a record of your credits and ensure that you graduate on time.

Directions: Use the form on the next page to help your student write in the credits for coursework completed. You will notice that the form is constructed for all subjects, as well as for two quarters. The State of California's minimum course requirements are entered under each subject.

*If your student resides in a different state, please check your state minimum course requirements for high school graduation, as each state's requirements will vary.

In the left column, the total number of credits needed per subject is left blank. Help your student identify this number. Each school district has the authority and responsibility to establish its own high school requirements—these usually exceed the state-mandated requirements.

Credit Planner

Student Directions: After reviewing your transcripts, enter the total number of credits needed for each subject in the left column. Also enter the completed credits per subject and quarter.

Credits Needed	Subject	Ninth Fall	Ninth Spring	Tenth Fall	Tenth Spring	Eleventh Fall	Eleventh Spring	Twelfth Fall	Twelfth Spring
_____	History Social Science 3 years								
_____	English 3 years								
_____	Mathematics 2 years								
_____	Science or Integrated Science 2 years								
_____	Language or Fine Arts 1 year								
_____	Physical Education 2 years								
_____	Electives								
___/___	Total Credits								

Check if applicable: ☐ Algebra 1 passed

Day 2

Exercise 3

INPUT

Coach Script: Being on time to class shows that you are responsible, organized, and have excellent time management skills. It also shows that you come to school ready to learn. These skills are important for success in any career or college. As part of your goal-setting program, you will be required to keep track of your attendance record each week. At the end of the 8-week program, you will see how often you were tardy, absent, or present in class.

Directions: Go over your student's attendance records with them. Next, have your student write down a goal on a blank sheet of paper using the example below. Be sure to make enough copies of the weekly class attendance record on the next page for each of your student's classes. Each page has 8 weeks. Your student should submit the records to you at the beginning of each week, starting on Week 2.

My Attendance Goals

I will try my best to be on time to school every day. I will only have _____ unexcused absences and _____ tardies by the end of my 8-week program.

Weekly Class Attendance Record

Name: Date:

Student Directions: Circle one of the following for your class each week.

Class_____ Teacher_____ Room#_____

T = Tardy   U = Unexcused Absence   E = Excused Absence   P = Present

Week	Monday	Tuesday	Wednesday	Thursday	Friday
Week 1	T U E P	T U E P	T U E P	T U E P	T U E P
Week 2	T U E P	T U E P	T U E P	T U E P	T U E P
Week 3	T U E P	T U E P	T U E P	T U E P	T U E P
Week 4	T U E P	T U E P	T U E P	T U E P	T U E P
Week 5	T U E P	T U E P	T U E P	T U E P	T U E P
Week 6	T U E P	T U E P	T U E P	T U E P	T U E P
Week 7	T U E P	T U E P	T U E P	T U E P	T U E P
Week 8	T U E P	T U E P	T U E P	T U E P	T U E P

Week 3

Organization and Time Management

Level 1 - Days 1 & 2	Week 3 of SCALE High Lesson Plan
SCALE Standards	**Standard 4:** List some areas that could use organization in their life (e.g., classes, schedules, etc.) and how he/she plans to get them in order **Standard 5:** Make a plan to manage time appropriately during the school week.
Anticipatory Set	Day 1- *Coach Script:* Do you know someone who is extremely organized? Describe them. What can you learn from them to help you become more organized? Show Week 3 video to your student. Day 2- *Coach Script:* Are you a punctual individual? If so, how are you punctual? If not, what are some things that you can do to make better use of your time?
Objective	Student will determine a study routine by constructing a time management study plan that they will use daily with at least 90% accuracy.
Essential Question	*Ask your student,* "How can you manage your time more wisely?"
Purpose	To help your student analyze levels of organization and time management.
Input	Day 1: You will facilitate **page 70.** Prior to the session, you will tell your student to bring their backpack and binder, and then you will implement **pages 28-29.** Day 2: You will administer **pages 30-31.**
Modeling	Demonstrate for your student how to appropriately organize a binder and backpack.
Check for Understanding	*Ask your student to give a thumbs up or thumbs down to the following statements:* Being organized will help you be more efficient in school. A daily planner will help you stay organized with your assignments. Having a study routine will help you manage your time.
Guided Practice (5-10 min)	Day 1: Have your student select supplies from the organization checklist. Day 2: Have your student calculate how well they manage their time, and help them construct a time management study plan.
Closure (EQ. Answer)	Answers may vary: organize school materials, set an alarm, make a schedule, create a weekly planner, set SMART goals, etc.
Independent Practice	Have your student select three pictures (online or from a magazine) to cut and place on their SCALE board for Week 8. Pictures should represent goals within SCALE High's first tier level: School.
Materials	SCALE High teaching manual, magazines, backpack and binder, copy of the "Student Organization Checklist," copy of "Exercise 5," copy of the "Time Management Study Plan," and a pencil.

Day 1

Exercise 4

INPUT

Coach Script: Organizational skills are life-long skills that can be learned and achieved with great practice. Some people are naturally organized and punctual, while others will need to work hard to get there. It is essential that you stay organized and manage your time wisely during and after school to pass your classes, study on time, and plan accordingly for graduation. Since you spend a good majority of your time at school, today you will learn how to keep your school binder organized. Many students have difficulty staying organized with their school materials, and they end up losing assignments or important paperwork. Being organized will allow you to catch up on late work as well as turn in assignments on time. Organizing your school materials will eventually lead to you being more organized in others areas of your life.

Directions: Have your student pull out their class binder. Look through the binder to check for organization or lack thereof. Be sure to express that you are trying to help them stay organized so they can be efficient in school. Help your student complete the exercises on the following pages.

Student Organization Checklist

Name: Date:

Student Directions: Go through your binder and check off every item that you have that is shown below. If you are missing any item from what you see below, make a list and a note to purchase these items so that you can be more efficient and organized in school.

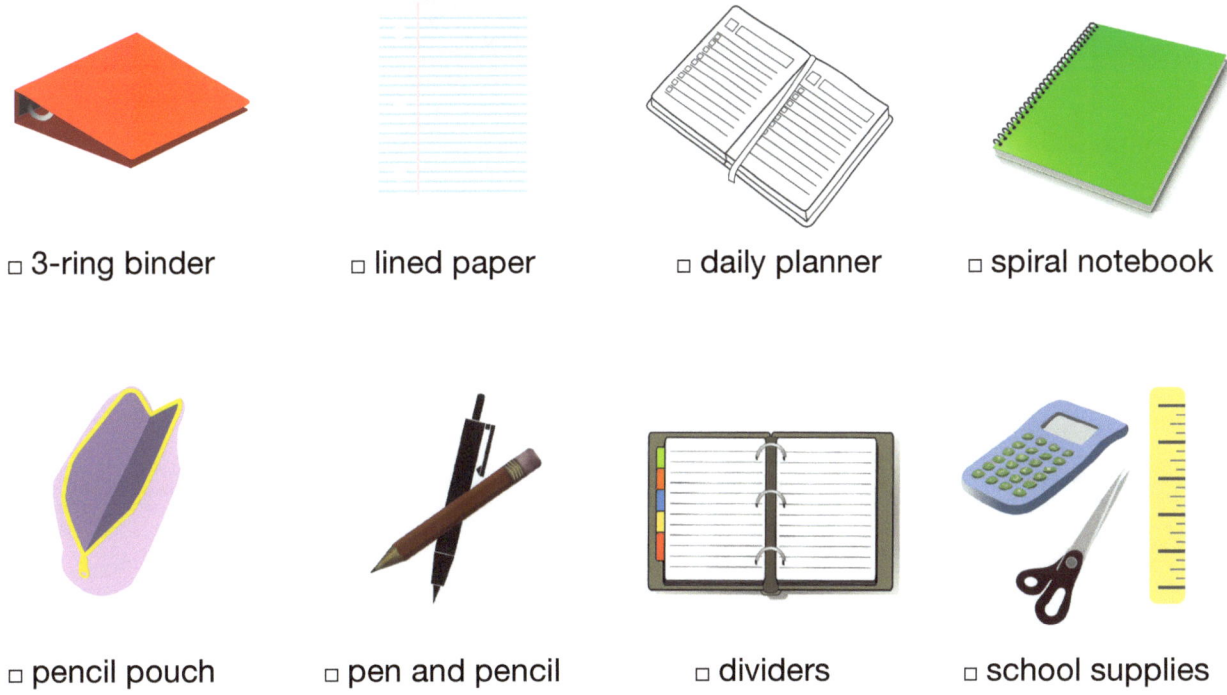

☐ 3-ring binder   ☐ lined paper   ☐ daily planner   ☐ spiral notebook

☐ pencil pouch   ☐ pen and pencil   ☐ dividers   ☐ school supplies

DON'T FORGET: Purchase a sturdy 3-ring binder that will last you the entire year. Be sure to place tabbed or color-coded dividers to separate your classes. Use pocket dividers to separate classwork, completed homework, and exams.

Keeping a daily planner will allow you to keep your homework assignments organized by due date, know when to study for an exam, and remember school events. Loose-leaf paper allows for easy use and access, while a spiral notebook can be used to take class notes. Decide what needs to stay in your binder and keep all other supplies in a supply box or pouch.

Day 2

How Well I Manage My Time

Name: Date:

Student Directions: How well do you manage your time when you need to study? Answer the following questions and use the scoring guide below to calculate your final score.

Agree = 3 points   Sometimes = 2 points   Disagree = 1 point

Affirmation	Points
I have successfully prepared a quiet place to study that has limited distractions.	
I have established a set schedule for the time that I will study every day after school.	
I have all my materials within reach in my study environment so I do not have to get up.	
I write my homework assignments in my daily planner or notebook, and check it regularly.	
I ask a knowledgeable person for help if I do not understand my assignment or homework.	
I do not wait until the last minute to study for exams, as I know it will not be beneficial to my success.	
I am responsible for bringing my textbooks home so I can successfully complete my homework.	
I have a binder with dividers so I can organize the materials for each of my classes, by period.	

Total Points _____

Check out your score!

If you scored:

- 18-24   **Five stars!** You have outstanding study skills. Keep up the great work!
- 9-17   **So-So:** You have some good habits, but you can learn more.
- 8   **Uh-Oh:** You could use some help with your study habits. Discuss with your Coach.

Time Management Study Plan

Name: Date:

Student Directions: Complete the exercise below. This is your opportunity to make a plan to better organize yourself and your time.

I have a quiet place to study.
☐ Yes   ☐ No

My quiet place at home will be *(indicate place)*:
_____

I have my study place set up.
☐ Yes   ☐ No

My study place will be set up by *(indicate date)*:
_____

The most practical time of day for me to study is *(check one)*:
☐ Morning   ☐ Afternoon   ☐ Evening   ☐ Night

I play sports or participate in extracurricular activities that cause my schedule to vary from day to day:
☐ Yes, it varies   ☐ It rarely varies   ☐ It does not vary

My study routine will be as follows *(indicate times)*:

Mondays from _____ to _____

Tuesdays from _____ to _____

Wednesdays from _____ to _____

Thursdays from _____ to _____

Fridays from _____ to _____

I will begin implementing my study routine on *(indicate date)*:
_____

I, _____ as a participant in the SCALE High Program, promise to adhere to my time management study plan throughout the school year in order to improve my organizational skills and study habits.

Level 2

Career

Build

5-year Goals

Career Options and Career Search

Week 4

Level 2 - Days 1 & 2	Week 4 of SCALE High Lesson Plan
SCALE Standards	**Standard 6:** Find time to learn how to: apply for a job; learn about the interview process; and how to create a resume and cover letter.
Anticipatory Set	Day 1- *Coach Script*: If you could choose any career, what would your dream career be? Show Week 4 video to your student. Day 2- *Coach Script:* Searching for a job can be overwhelming, but having the right information and learning how to search for a job will help alleviate some of that stress.
Objective	Student will identify three possible career choices by fully completing the "My Dream Career" worksheet.
Essential Question	*Ask your student,* "What is the difference between a job and a career?"
Purpose	To identify your student's possible career choices.
Input	Day 1: Coach facilitates page 70. Coach guides student as they add six goals to the Career column on page 19. Coach administers pages 35-36. Day 2: Coach facilitates pages 37-38.
Modeling	Coach will demonstrate how to use www.caljobs.ca.gov to do a quick job and career search.
Check for Understanding	**4-3-2-1 Scoring Scale-** *Coach Script:* Using your fingers, on a scale of 1 to 4 (4 being "I understand" and 1 being "I am confused"), how are you doing with your career search?
Guided Practice (5-10 min)	Day 1: Student identifies top three career choices. Day 2: Student chooses one career from the top three choices to research on www.caljobs.ca.gov.
Closure (EQ. Answer)	A job is a short-term activity that you do for income. A career is a life-long pursuit of a life-long dream. *Note: your student's answer may vary along these lines.*
Independent Practice	Student is to select three pictures (online or from a magazine) to cut and place on their SCALE board for Week 8. Pictures should represent goals within SCALE High's second tier level: Career.
Materials	SCALE High teaching manual, magazines, computer, original copy of "Exercise 1," copy of "My Dream Career," copy of "My Job and Career Search," and a pencil.

Day 1

Exercise 6

INPUT

Ask your student: Have you ever imagined what your dream career looks like? What career do you picture yourself doing for the rest of your life? How does that career make you feel? How do you plan on accomplishing your goals to get there?

By answering some of these questions, you will start the process of finding out what you are truly passionate about, and the steps you need to take to turn your dream into a reality. Now I am going to ask you some career choice questions. Answer as truthfully as possible.

Career Choice Questions

1) What are you good at doing?

2) What do you enjoy doing? Do you ever get bored doing it?

3) How does it make you feel? Can you spend the next 20-40 years doing it?

4) Who or what influences your career choice? (e.g., money, location, family, etc.)

5) Where are you now, and how do you plan to achieve your dream career?

My Dream Career

Student Directions: List three activities you enjoy doing and state why you enjoy doing them. Then list three possible careers you would be interested in pursuing.

List three activities that you enjoy doing and never get tired of doing:

I enjoy _____
because _____

I enjoy _____
because _____

I enjoy _____
because _____

List your top three possible career choices and explain why you like them:

1) _____
   _____
   _____

2) _____
   _____
   _____

3) _____
   _____
   _____

Day 2

Exercise 7

INPUT

Ask your student: Have you ever searched for a job? If so, what website, temp agency, or newspaper classifieds did you use? There are plenty of resources out there to help you find a job or career. Notice I said *job* or *career*. Though these words are often used interchangeably, there is a difference between the two.

A job is a short-term activity that you do to earn money. A job may or may not require special education or training, and usually feels more like work rather than something you enjoy doing.

A career is a long-term pursuit of a life-long dream. In a career, you can build up your skills towards higher pay and prestige position opportunities. A career takes goal-setting, special training, education, and usually doesn't feel like work because you're doing something that you're passionate about.

The following are just a few examples of websites you can use to search for a job or career: craigslist.org, monster.com, careerbuilder.com, indeed.com, job.com, theladders.com, simplyhired.com, resumerabbit.com, and caljobs.ca.gov.

There are plenty of others; however, today we will be using CalJobs. Let's get started.

Note: If you reside in a state other than California, use an appropriate job site for your state.

My Job and Career Search

Name: Date:

Student Directions: You will use the CalJobs site to seek potential job or career choices. Type www.caljobs.ca.gov in your web browser and follow the steps below.

Write down your answers for one (1) job search and keep it in your folder, to be used later. Repeat the steps below for two other searches.

Note: The layout of the website may change over time.

- **Home Page:** on the left side of the webpage, click *"Find a Job."*

- **Quick Job Search:** in the *"Search Criteria"* box, enter a keyword that describes the career title you are interested in (e.g., police officer), then click "Search."

- **Summary:** you will be shown a summary of jobs in your area. Each summary will list: Job Title / Description Snippet; Employer; Location; and Salary. Click on the "Detailed" tab to the right of "Results View" (at the top) to read additional details of each position.

- **Job Details:** scroll down to view the list of jobs, then click on any of the highlighted job titles to view additional information.

- **Job Summary/Job Description:** scroll down the page to view and read the following:

    a)   Job Title
    b)   Employer Name
    c)   City, State, Zip
    d)   Date the Job Posted
    e)   Positions Available
    f)   Occupation
    g)   Job Requirements
    h)   Job Properties
    i)   Salary
    j)   Job Description
    k)   Additional Information

- Click the "Home" button in the upper left corner, and repeat the steps for two more keywords.

Application and Mock Interview

Level 2 - Days 1 & 2	Week 5 of SCALE High Lesson Plan
SCALE Standards	**Standard 6:** Find time to learn how to: apply for a job; learn about the interview process; and how to create a resume and cover letter **Standard 6.1:** Practice a mock interview with an adult
Anticipatory Set	Day 1- *Coach Script*: Last week you learned how to do a career search. Today you will learn how to apply for that dream career you have always wanted. Show Week 5 video to student. Day 2- *Coach Script*: Preparing for a job interview can be nerve-racking. Today you will learn how to prepare for an interview and get some tips on what to ask or say during the interview.
Objective	Student will summarize the application process and perform as an applicant by completing a mock interview with 90% accuracy.
Essential Question	*Ask your student,* "What two supporting documents will you need to submit with a job application?"
Purpose	To demonstrate your student's knowledge of the application process and perform a mock interview.
Input	Day 1: You will facilitate **pages 69-70** and then explain **pages 41-43**. Next, you will use **page 42** to help your student create a resume (handwritten or typed). Day 2: You will administer **pages 44-45.**
Modeling	You will demonstrate the job interview process and facilitate a mock interview.
Check for Understanding	**Entrance / Exit Ticket:** Give your student a ticket to complete before leaving the session. The ticket asks: *What is the most important thing you have learned today? What questions do you still have?* Collect the ticket either at the end of the session or the beginning of the next session.
Guided Practice (5-10 min)	Day 1: Have your student summarize the application and interview process. Day 2: Have your student perform a mock interview.
Closure (EQ. Answer)	When submitting a job application, most companies will request a cover letter and resume as supporting documents. Both documents give employers a preview of your background experience, skills, and personality.
Independent Practice	Have your student select three pictures (online or from a magazine) to cut and place on their SCALE board for Week 8. Pictures should represent goals within SCALE High's second tier level: Career.
Materials	SCALE High teaching manual, magazines, mock interview outfit (tell your student to dress professionally), your student's resume, and a pencil.

Day 1

Exercise 8

INPUT

Coach Script: The first step towards obtaining your dream career is knowing how to navigate the application process, and learning the essential steps to get your foot in the door.

9 Steps to Navigate the Application Process

Step 1: **Decide what type of job you want** – consider requirements, skills, and salary.

Step 2: **Research** the company you are applying to before you apply.

Step 3: **Create a resume** with current contact information, updated skills, education, and work history.

Step 4: **Begin the application process** – be sure to carefully read all the instructions for the application process if you are applying online, or contact the employer to request information on how to apply.

Step 5: **Prepare a cover letter** – stay away from mass emailing. Instead, write your letter specifically for the company and job you're applying for.

Step 6: **Review and edit** – ask friends and family to help polish your resume and cover letter.

Step 7: **Collect references** – provide at least three references: two should be individuals with whom you have worked with in the past, who can speak regarding your job performance.

Step 8: **Apply** to your job in person, online, or by mail, ensuring all necessary documents are enclosed or attached.

Step 9: **Follow up** one to two weeks after you have submitted your application. This shows that you are interested in the job. Be sure to call only after the job close date (if listed).

Sample Resume

John Doe
10 Highland Avenue
Long Beach, CA 90804
(555) 555-5555
john.doe@myemail.com

Education   Highland Park High School, class of 2017 (3.9 GPA)

Experience
Long Beach Grill—Busboy (August 2016 - present)
- Cleaned tabletops and ensured that fresh tablecloths and mats are placed
- Provided waiters or waitresses with information of new customer arrival
- Organized and cleaned dishes in the kitchen and expedited orders
- Assisted customers looking for service

National Honor Society—Volunteer Assistant (2015 - present)
Participated in numerous volunteer activities, including:
- Building a house for Habitat for Humanity (30 hours)
- Collecting food for Meals on Wheels (50 hours)
- Organizing events for the National Honor Society

Activities
- Chess Club (4 years)—participated in state and national tournaments
- Yearbook Club (3 years)—coordinated layout and content

Skills
- Strong interpersonal skills, oral, and written communication skills
- Customer service skills
- Ability to work as part of a team and follow instructions
- Ability to incorporate technology (Microsoft Office, social media)

References
Available upon request

Contact Information: place this at the top of your resume, in the center with bold font. Include: name, address, phone number, and email.

Education: include school, graduation date, and GPA (if it is 3.0 or higher).

Experience: include title and dates followed by a bulleted or narrative list. Begin each bullet with an active verb (e.g., coordinated, organized, participated).

Activities: list your academic, school, and extracurricular activities.

Skills: a good way to find the skills you need for the job is to check the job requirements in the job positing. Otherwise, use the general skills that you possess.

Sample Cover Letter

John Doe
10 Highland Avenue
Long Beach, CA 90804
(555) 555-5555
john.doe@myemail.com

April 15, 2017

Ms. Dupé R. Aleru
5541 E. 7th Street
Long Beach, CA 90804

Dear Ms. Aleru,

I am applying for the in-home tutoring position as advertised on BeachLink, via California State University, Long Beach website. I have experience tutoring in mathematics and I think I would be a great addition to your tutoring organization.

I was a peer tutor at my former high school for four years, tutoring Algebra I through Calculus III. In all my mathematics courses—including the AP courses—I received a B letter grade or higher.

My desire is to be able to add value to Tutors for Tots. I admire how your organization has been helping students achieve academic success since 2010.

I hope that you will consider me for the position. You may contact me by phone (555) 555-5555 or by email john.doe@myemail.com.

I look forward to speaking with you to discuss my experience and how I can be of benefit to Tutors for Tots, Tweens & Teens LLC.

Sincerely,

John Doe

---

1 Contact Information: the first section or header should include your: name, address, phone number (or cellphone number), and email address.

2 Date: use the current date that you are sending the email, fax, or letter.

3 Return Address: do your research to find the return address of the employer.

4 Salutation: find out the name of the individual you're sending the letter. Try to avoid, "To Whom It May Concern" as it may look unprofessional; like you didn't put in the effort.

5 Body: 1st paragraph: why you are writing; 2nd paragraph: what you have to offer the employer; 3rd paragraph: your knowledge of the company; 4th paragraph: your closing.

6 Closing: complimentary closing.

7 Signature: type your name then sign your name (scanned or an image).

Day 2

Exercise 9

INPUT

Coach Script: Preparing for a job interview can be exciting and terrifying at the same time. You have one chance to make a great first impression on an employer, and knowing exactly what to wear, what to say, and how to conduct yourself during the interview can give you an edge over the other applicants, who may or may not have more experience than you do. Listen closely as I go over some interview pointers.

Tip: Show a video on appropriate job interview attire. YouTube has a collection of videos. Search "What to wear to a job interview," and choose a video you like.

Before the Interview
- **Research the company** – know as much as possible about the company, including the interviewer's name, before you walk through the doors.
- **Ask questions** – asking questions and participating during the interview gives the impression that you are interested, so be sure to make your list beforehand.
- **Mock interview** – practice a mock interview with an adult. Be sure to make eye contact and give clear answers to any questions asked.
- **Anticipate questions** – go over potential interview questions that the interviewer may ask you (e.g., your strengths and weaknesses).

Day of the Interview
- **Dress to impress** – showing up formally dressed or in business casual is always best. Be sure to iron your clothes and look presentable.
- **Be punctual** – an old saying goes, "If you're on time, you're late." Be sure to arrive 10-15 minutes before your scheduled interview time.
- **Bring materials** – always have on hand an extra copy of your resume and cover letter, in addition to references, letters of recommendation, and any certifications that might be beneficial to the position to which you are applying.

During the Interview
- **Be courteous** – greet everyone at the location and use good manners.
- **Be personable** – show off your personality, but keep greetings short and simple.

After the Interview
- **Thank your interviewer** – shake hands with the interviewer and later send a thank you card or email; and follow up in two weeks.

Mock Interview

Directions: Prior to today's session, request that your student come dressed appropriately for the mock interview. Encourage your student to bring their resume from "Exercise 8."

Give your student 2 to 5 minutes to come up with some interview questions to ask you (the employer) during the interview. Lastly, prompt your student to answer the following questions based upon the job they researched during "Exercise 7."

Coach: Thank you for being on time. Good morning/afternoon, my name is _____ and I will be conducting your interview today.
Shake your student's hand.
Please have a seat.

Coach: We are interviewing you for the position of _____. We are looking for someone who is excited about this opportunity and who is looking to grow within our organization. This individual should also be dependable, professional, and be able to get along well with others.

Questions you can ask your student:

- Did you bring a copy of your resume? *(Allow student to hand it to you)*

- Tell me a little about yourself. *(Pause and give time to answer)*

- What are some of your strengths? *(Pause and give time to answer)*

- What are some your weaknesses? *(Pause and give time to answer)*

- Why does this job interest you? *(Pause and give time to answer)*

- I noticed that you put on your application that you have special skills. Do you mind elaborating? *(Pause and give time to answer)*

- Tell me about your most recent job. *(If they have never held a job, have them talk about helping a family member or a volunteer experience)*

- Why did you leave your last job? *(If they have never held a job, ask them why they are looking for work now)*

- Do you have any questions for me? *(Pause and give time to answer)*

Coach: It was a pleasure meeting with you today. We will be in touch soon.

Week 6

Paths to College and Financial Aid

Level 2 - Days 1 & 2	Week 6 of SCALE High Lesson Plan
SCALE Standards	**Standard 7:** Demonstrate knowledge about the various college systems: 2-year college, 4-year university, and graduate school **Standard 8:** Make a personal commitment to learn about financial aid and grants **Standard 9:** Monitor short-term school goals in regards to graduation
Anticipatory Set	Day 1- *Coach Script:* Do you know the various college systems? This week you will learn what each system has to offer. Show Week 6 video to your student. Day 2- *Coach Script:* Financial aid and grants can help alleviate financial stress and burden while attending college. Today we will go over the different types of financial aid and grants available to students.
Objective	Student will restate the various college systems and their requirements by completing the "Path to College Quiz" with 100% accuracy.
Essential Question	*Ask your student,* "Can you name more than two different college systems?"
Purpose	To identify the various college systems and types of financial aid/grants available to students.
Input	Day 1: Facilitate page 70 and then administer pages 48-50. Answer key for page 50 is on page 73. Day 2: Administer pages 51-52. Answer key for page 52 is on page 75.
Modeling	Teach the various paths to college and explain the types of financial aid/grants available to your student.
Check for Understanding	**Example/Non-Example:** Give a concept and have your student state examples or non-examples. *Example:* My friend would like to attend a 4-year university, give her two options.
Guided Practice (5-10 min)	Day 1: Student will evaluate their knowledge of the various college systems. Day 2: Student will evaluate their knowledge of different types of financial aid and grants.
Closure (EQ. Answer)	Community college or junior college; CSU or California State University; UC or University of California; vocational, technical, or career colleges.
Independent Practice	Have your student select three pictures (online or from a magazine) to cut and place on their SCALE board for Week 8. Pictures should represent goals within SCALE High's second tier level: Career.
Materials	SCALE High teaching manual, magazines, copy of "Path to College Quiz," copy of "Financial Aid Crossword Puzzle," and a pencil.

Day 1

Exercise 10

INPUT

Coach Script: Examine the different paths you can take to get to college.

For additional information, refer to the handouts on **pages 71-72.**

Graduate School

- Master's Program
- Ph.D. Program
- Professional Program (e.g., Law)

2-Year College

- Community College or Junior College (JC)
- Technical College, Vocational College, or Career College

4-Year University

- University of California (UC)
- California State University (CSU)

High School

- Traditional Public School
- Traditional Private School
- Charter, Magnet, or Montessori

Paths to College

	UC	CSU	Community College
Number of Campuses in California	9	23 on-campus 8 off-campus	113
Degrees Awarded	• Bachelor • Masters • Ph.D. • Professional • Credentials	• Bachelor • Masters • Ph.D. • Credentials	• Associates' • Certificates
A-G Requirements	YES	YES	NO
SAT or ACT	YES	YES	NO
Minimum G.P.A	3.0 (3.4 non-residents)	2.0 (minimum test scores required)	H.S. Diploma

Paths to College Quiz

Name: Date:

1. Can you obtain a Ph.D. at a California State University (CSU)?   ☐ Yes ☐ No

2. Do most Community Colleges require you to take the SAT or ACT?   ☐ Yes ☐ No

3. What is the highest level of education a person can obtain?
   ☐   Associate degree (A.A.)
   ☐   High school diploma
   ☐   Master's degree (M.A., M.S., M.F.A.)
   ☐   Doctoral or professional degree (Ph.D., J.D., M.D.)
   ☐   Bachelor's degree (B.A., B.S.)

4. The following are either part of a 2-year college or 4-year university system. Check the one that does not apply:
   ☐   University of California
   ☐   California State University
   ☐   Vocational College
   ☐   Magnet School
   ☐   Career College

5. The A-G requirements are classes you must take and pass in order to:
   ☐   Graduate from high school
   ☐   Get into graduate school
   ☐   Get accepted to a University of California (UC) or California State University (CSU)
   ☐   Take the SAT or ACT
   ☐   Gain acceptance into a trade school

Day 2

Exercise 11

INPUT

Coach Script: Financial aid offers to help students meet their college expenses. There are four basic types of financial aid available. Students can use the Free Application for Federal Student Aid (FAFSA) form to help determine their eligibility for student financial aid. *For additional information, refer to the handout on* **page 74.**

Four Types of Financial Aid

Scholarships	Grants	Loans	Employment
• Private monies • No repayment	• Federal Grants according to financial need, through FASFA • State Grants for CA residents only	• Federal Loans you must repay • Private Loans, credit-based loans to help bridge the gap on the amount you owe	• Federal Work Study • Federally funded • Limited placements

Financial Aid Crossword Puzzle

Student Directions: Fill out the crossword puzzle using the clues below. If you need assistance, refer back to your manual that defined the four types of financial aid.

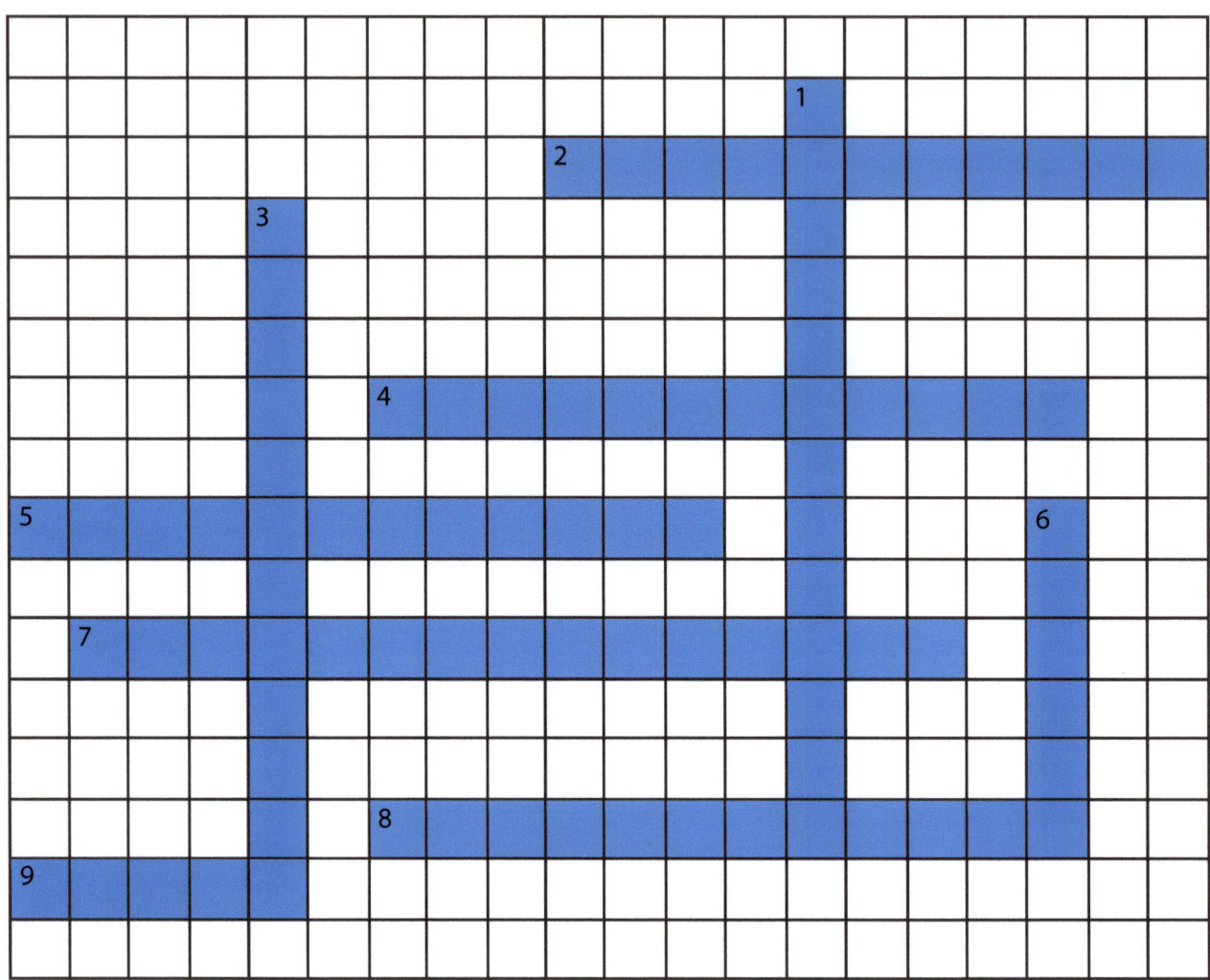

Word Bank

☐ private loans ☐ scholarships ☐ grants ☐ loans ☐ federal grants
☐ employment loans ☐ state grants ☐ financial aid ☐ federal loans

Across
2. For state residents only
4. Helps students meet their college expenses
5. Credit-based loans that help bridge the gap
7. A federal work-study that's federally funded
8. Private money that you don't have to pay back
9. Federal and private types offered

Down
1. Based on your financial needs
3. Loans you must pay back
6. Federal and state types offered

Life

BIG Picture

10-year Goals

Level 3

Week 7

School Mirrors the Workplace and Recap

Level 3 - Days 1 & 2	Week 7 of SCALE High Lesson Plan
SCALE Standards	**Standard 3.1:** Identify and understand how certain aspects of school mirror the workplace and world
Anticipatory Set	Day 1- *Coach Script:* What comes to mind when you hear the phrase, "School mirrors the workplace?" (Pause and allow student to respond). Today, you will learn how school is a reflection of how the workplace operates. Show Week 7 video to student. Day 2- *Coach Script:* We are getting close to the end of our program. It has been fun getting to know you and learning about your goals, and how you plan on achieving them. Today we will recap on what you have learned so far.
Objective	Student will explore how school is a reflection of the workplace by completing the "School Mirrors the Workplace" activity with 100% accuracy.
Essential Question	*Ask your student,* "How is a principal at a school similar to a boss at a workplace?"
Purpose	To explore how school mirrors the workplace.
Input	Day 1: Facilitate page 70 and administer pages 56-57. Day 2: Administer pages 58-59.
Modeling	List the ways in which school mirrors the workplace.
Check for Understanding	**Thumbs Up/Thumbs Down:** Remind your student that they should have good attendance at school and work. Remind them that it is important to manage their time at both, though your student might not need to set specific goals at work.
Guided Practice (5-10 min)	Day 1: Student will explore how school mirrors the workplace. Day 2: Student will summarize their SCALE High experience.
Closure (EQ. Answer)	*Possible answers-* They are both: leaders; enforce a positive learning environment; give a form of compensation for hard work; provide positive reinforcement; reinforce policies and procedures to follow; allow creativity.
Independent Practice	Your student should select two pictures (online or from a magazine) to cut and place on their SCALE board for Week 8. Pictures should represent goals within SCALE High's third tier level: Life.
Materials	SCALE High teaching manual, magazines, copy of "School Mirrors the Workplace," copy of "My SCALE High Experience," and a pencil.

Day 1

Exercise 12

INPUT

Student Directions: Take a look at how school mirrors the world. Feel free to add any other suggestions to the list. Next, we will see how school mirrors the workplace.

School Mirrors the Real World

- Set goals
- Manage time
- Be punctual
- Positive attitude
- Respect those around you
- Listen to authority
- Be present

- Set goals
- Manage time
- Be punctual
- Positive attitude
- Respect those around you
- Listen to authority
- Be present

School Mirrors the Workplace

Name: Date:

Student Directions: School mirrors the workplace in many ways. See if you can figure out the similarities and discuss them with your Coach. Identify the similarities by placing the *letters* in the left column on the correct *lines* in the right column.

School   **Workplace**

a. Principal   _____ Coworkers
b. School Rules   _____ Job Applications
c. Peers   _____ Employee
d. Attendance Records   _____ Workplace
e. College Applications   _____ Policies & Procedure
f. Student   _____ Resume
g. Cumulative Files   _____ Employer
h. Classroom   _____ Time Sheets

Day 2

Exercise 13

INPUT

Coach Script: We are so close to the end of our program. Next week, we will spend the entire week putting together your SCALE board, but for now let's recap all the important information you have learned during the past seven weeks.

Let's Recap

- Identify your gifts and talents.
- Create a high school credit planner to keep track of your school credits.
- Come to school every day ready to learn, and try to have good attendance.
- Organizational and time management skills are life-long skills, so it is important to learn them early before you start your career.
- Keep your school materials organized in your class binders and backpack.
- Have a standard place and time to study every day.
- Start brainstorming and researching possible careers that interest you.
- Learn how to create a resume and cover letter.
- Master the steps to navigating the application process.
- Thoroughly prepare for your job interview.
- Perform a mock interview with an adult to practice the interview process.
- There are many different paths that you can take to go to college. Familiarize yourself with the various college systems and choose the path that best suits you.
- Be knowledgeable of the A-G requirements.
- Know your options for financial aid and grants.
- Understand that school mirrors the workplace. Therefore, it is imperative to take school seriously to set yourself up for success during your career.

My SCALE High Experience

Name: Date:

Student Directions: Take a few moments to think about your SCALE High experience and consider how the program has impacted your life—we hope it did. Do you feel more motivated? Have you made plans to speak with a counselor about your credits, graduation, or career options? Use the space below to talk about your experience and your future goal-setting plans.

Things I did not know, but I am now informed about are: _____
_____
_____
_____

My favorite part of the program was: _____
_____
_____
_____

The goals that I will get started on right away are: _____
_____
_____
_____

An "Ah-Ha" moment I had was when: _____
_____
_____
_____
_____

One important thing I will take away from this program is: _____
_____

Week 8

SCALE Board and Exit Survey

Level 3 - Days 1 & 2	Week 8 of SCALE High Lesson Plan
SCALE Standards	**Standard 1.3:** Identify steps to achieve and maintain 1-2 year, 5-year, and 10-year goals **Standard 1.4:** Develop a visual representation of these goals **Standard 10:** Monitor progress towards a life goal
Anticipatory Set	Day 1- *Coach Script:* Creating your SCALE board will help you envision where you want to be, and what you want to achieve at your 1-2 year, 5-year, and 10-year goal marks. Now it's time to put it all together. Show Week 8 video to student. Day 2- *Coach Script:* Can you see the finish line? How do you feel about your accomplishment? You did a tremendous job during our 8-week program. Now let's take a look at your SCALE board.
Objective	Student will illustrate a visual representation of their 1-2 year, 5-year, and 10-year goals by constructing a SCALE board with 100% accuracy.
Essential Question	*Ask your student,* "What is goal-setting? Describe the meaning in your own words."
Purpose	To illustrate a visual representation of your student's 1-, 5-, and 10-year goals.
Input	Day 1: Facilitate **page 70** and guide students as they add six goals to the Life column on **page 19.** Administer **pages 62-63.** Day 2: Administer **page 18 (post-test).** Then administer **pages 64-65.**
Modeling	Demonstrate how to create a SCALE board, using your own example.
Check for Understanding	Fill in your thoughts: My 1-2 year goal is _____. My 5-year goal is _____. My 10-year goal is _____. *Have your student choose one goal for each.*
Guided Practice (5-10 min)	Day 1: Have your student illustrate their SCALE board. Day 2: Have your student finish illustrating the SCALE board and complete the exit survey.
Closure (EQ. Answer)	*Possible answer:* Goal-setting is the process during which someone identifies something they want to accomplish and establishes a timeframe and measurable goals to achieve it.
Independent Practice	Your student can gather more items (online or from a magazine) to cut and place on their SCALE board. Pictures can represent their goals within all SCALE High's tier levels: School, Career, and Life.
Materials	SCALE High teaching manual, magazines, "Exercise 1," copy of "Steps to Achieve My Goals," copy of "Goal-Setting Questionnaire," access to "SCALE High Exit Survey," and a pencil.

Day 1

Exercise 14

INPUT

Coach Script: Let's get started putting together your SCALE board. Follow the steps below to help organize your board.

1. Use a cork board, cardboard, Styrofoam, or any hard surface as the foundation for your board.
2. Include a title. Print the title and glue it to your board. Or use foam letters with adhesive backing to display your title.
3. Create lines on your board or imagine lines to keep pictures organized within each tier level (School, Career, Life).
4. Tape or glue each picture as a collage.
5. Start from the bottom (Tier 1) and work your way up to the top (Tier 3).
6. Write the words "1-2 year," "5-year," and "10-year" near your lines. You can type and print these headers out.

Example of a SCALE board:

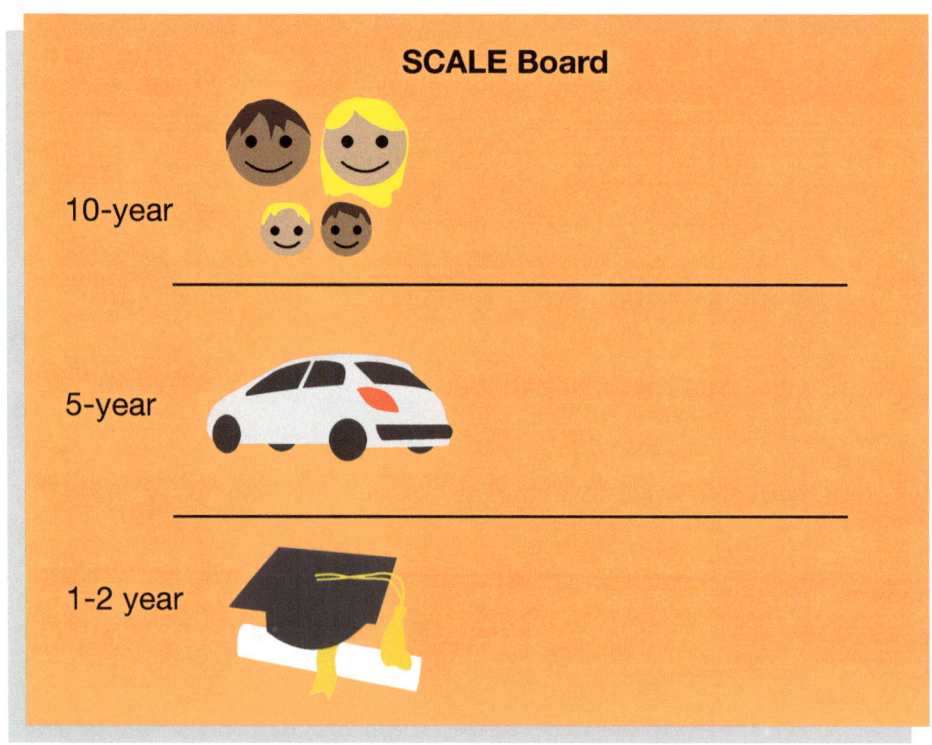

Steps to Achieve My Goals

Name: Date:

Student Directions: Choose *two* goals from each tier in "Exercise 1." Use the space below to write down the steps you need to take to achieve these goals.

Steps needed to achieve my 1-2 year goals:

- _____
  _____
  _____

- _____
  _____
  _____

Steps needed to achieve my 5-year goals:

- _____
  _____
  _____

- _____
  _____
  _____

Steps needed to achieve my 10-year goals:

- _____
  _____
  _____

- _____
  _____
  _____

Day 2

Exercise 15

INPUT

Coach Script: Continue where you left off this week and finish placing your pictures on your SCALE board. Your finished SCALE board should look similar to the one below. Feel free to place your pictures closer together as a collage, or keep them spaced apart.

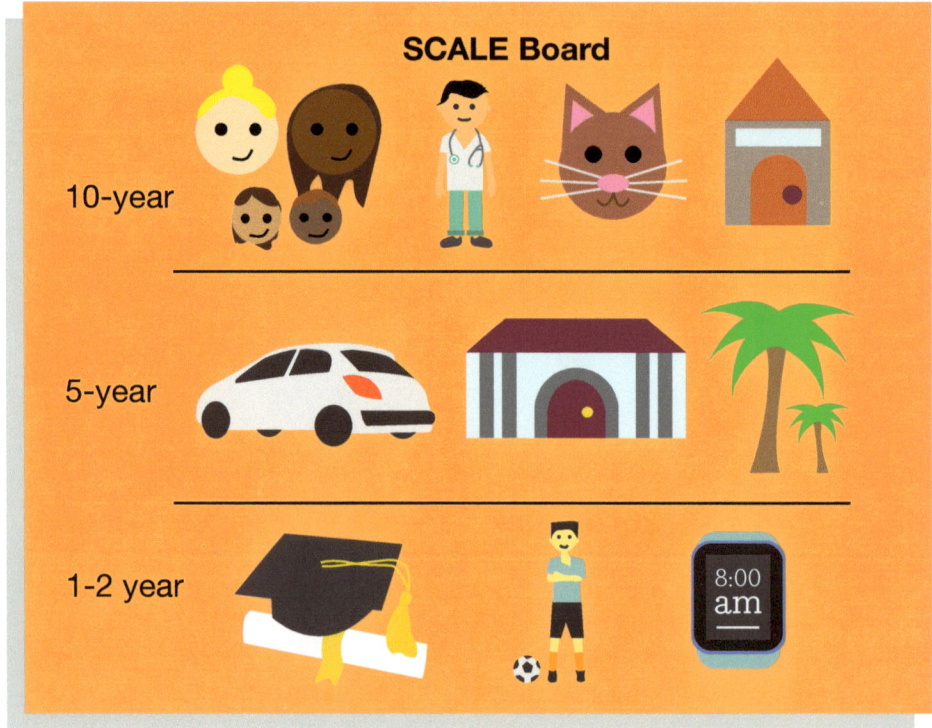

SCALE High Exit Survey

Student Directions: SCALE High needs your help. We kindly request that you complete the following Exit Survey at https://www.surveymonkey.com/r/5WGD8CR after you complete the SCALE High Program. Thank you in advance for your time and feedback. *Note: Questions are subject to change and may not appear as the ones listed below, so please use the online link.*

1. After completing this program, I feel prepared to start on my 1-2 year goal-setting journey.
   - ☐ Highly Disagree
   - ☐ Disagree
   - ☐ Neither Agree nor Disagree
   - ☐ Agree
   - ☐ Highly Agree

2. I developed useful goal-setting strategies and information that will help me succeed in school and life.
   - ☐ Highly Disagree
   - ☐ Disagree
   - ☐ Neither Agree nor Disagree
   - ☐ Agree
   - ☐ Highly Agree

3. My coach demonstrated knowledge of the program material, and made each session interesting and fun.
   - ☐ Highly Disagree
   - ☐ Disagree
   - ☐ Neither Agree nor Disagree
   - ☐ Agree
   - ☐ Highly Agree

4. My coach was effectively able to answer all of my questions and give me useful advice.
   - ☐ Highly Disagree
   - ☐ Disagree
   - ☐ Neither Agree nor Disagree
   - ☐ Agree
   - ☐ Highly Agree

5. The exercises given each week contributed to my learning and overall experience.
   - ☐ Highly Disagree
   - ☐ Disagree
   - ☐ Neither Agree nor Disagree
   - ☐ Agree
   - ☐ Highly Agree

6. I would recommend this program to a friend because I found it to be very beneficial for my success.
   - ☐ Yes
   - ☐ No

In Closing

Coach Script:

The SCALE High Program was specifically designed to inspire high school students like yourself as you develop a roadmap that will help you become successful in all walks of life. The purpose of the 8-week program is to have you explore what you desire to achieve from school, a career, and in life. By completing this program, we hope that you will start to envision what you want to accomplish in these three areas, and take action to achieve your goals.

As your coach, I would like to congratulate you on your achievement and dedication to completing the program. I wish you the best of luck in everything you set out to do. I hope you use the tools and skills that you learned in this program to reach new heights. As you go through life, my hope is that you keep your SCALE board as a reminder to *scale high* and continue on your journey towards living the life you are meant to live.

Handouts, Data, and Templates

Resources

Week 1

Students must complete a goal before moving on to the next goal.

Name:

Quarterly SMART Goals for

Start Date:

Directions: Circle one of the following: **academic, behavior, attendance.**
                                          Teacher   Counselor   Secretary

SMART goals for success!

S - Specific   Know what you want to achieve!
M - Measurable   How will you know when you reach your goal?
A - Achievable   What steps will you take to reach your goal?
R - Realistic   Set goals you are able to accomplish.
T - Timely   How long will it take to reach your goal?

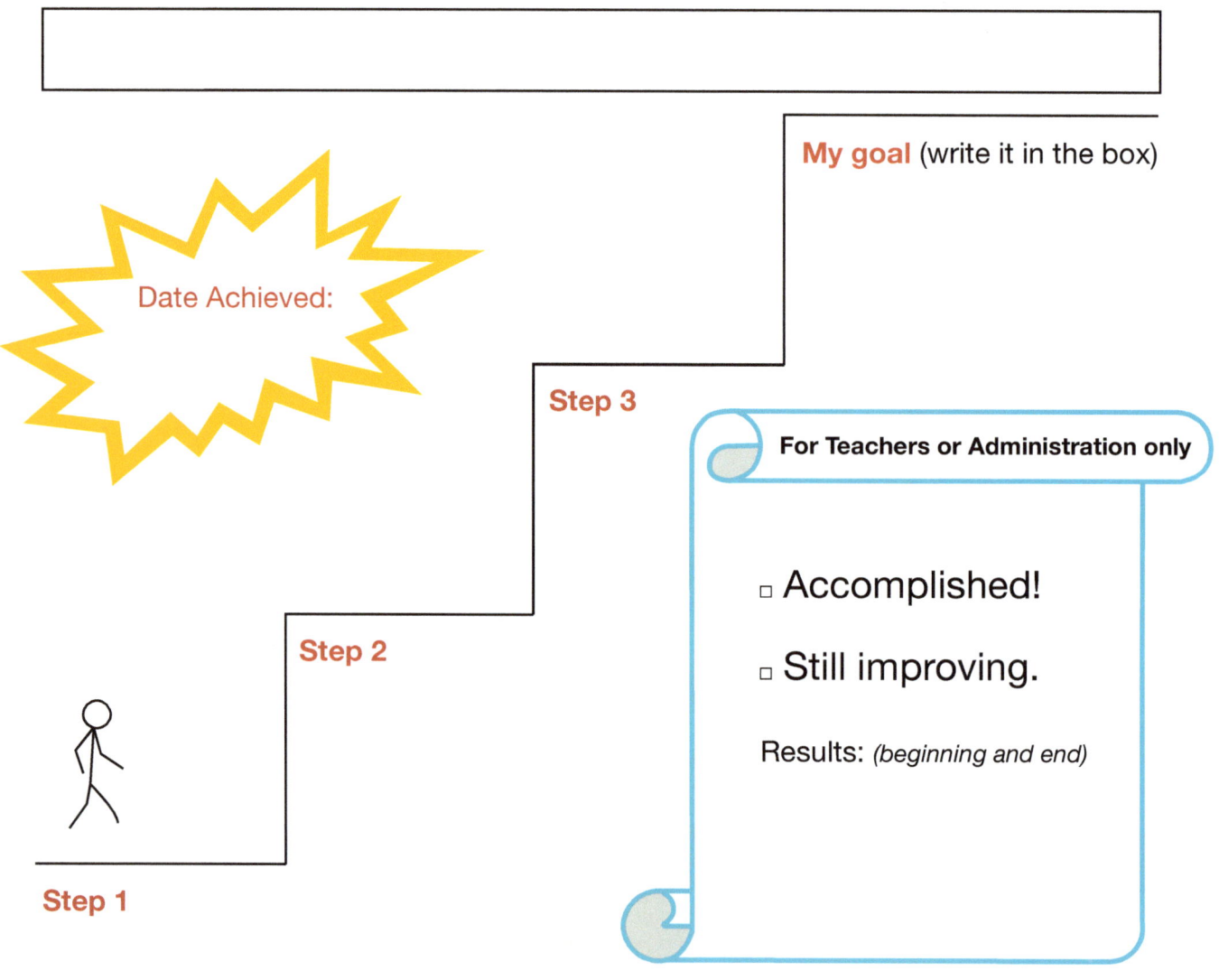

My goal (write it in the box)

Date Achieved:

Step 3

Step 2

Step 1

For Teachers or Administration only

☐ Accomplished!

☐ Still improving.

Results: (beginning and end)

68

Week 1 & 5

Students must complete a goal before moving on to the next goal.

Name:

Monthly SMART Goals for

Start Date:

Directions: Circle one of the following: **academic, behavior, attendance.**
Teacher   Counselor   Secretary

SMART goals for success!

S - Specific — Know what you want to achieve!
M - Measurable — How will you know when you reach your goal?
A - Achievable — What steps will you take to reach your goal?
R - Realistic — Set goals you are able to accomplish.
T - Timely — How long will it take to reach your goal?

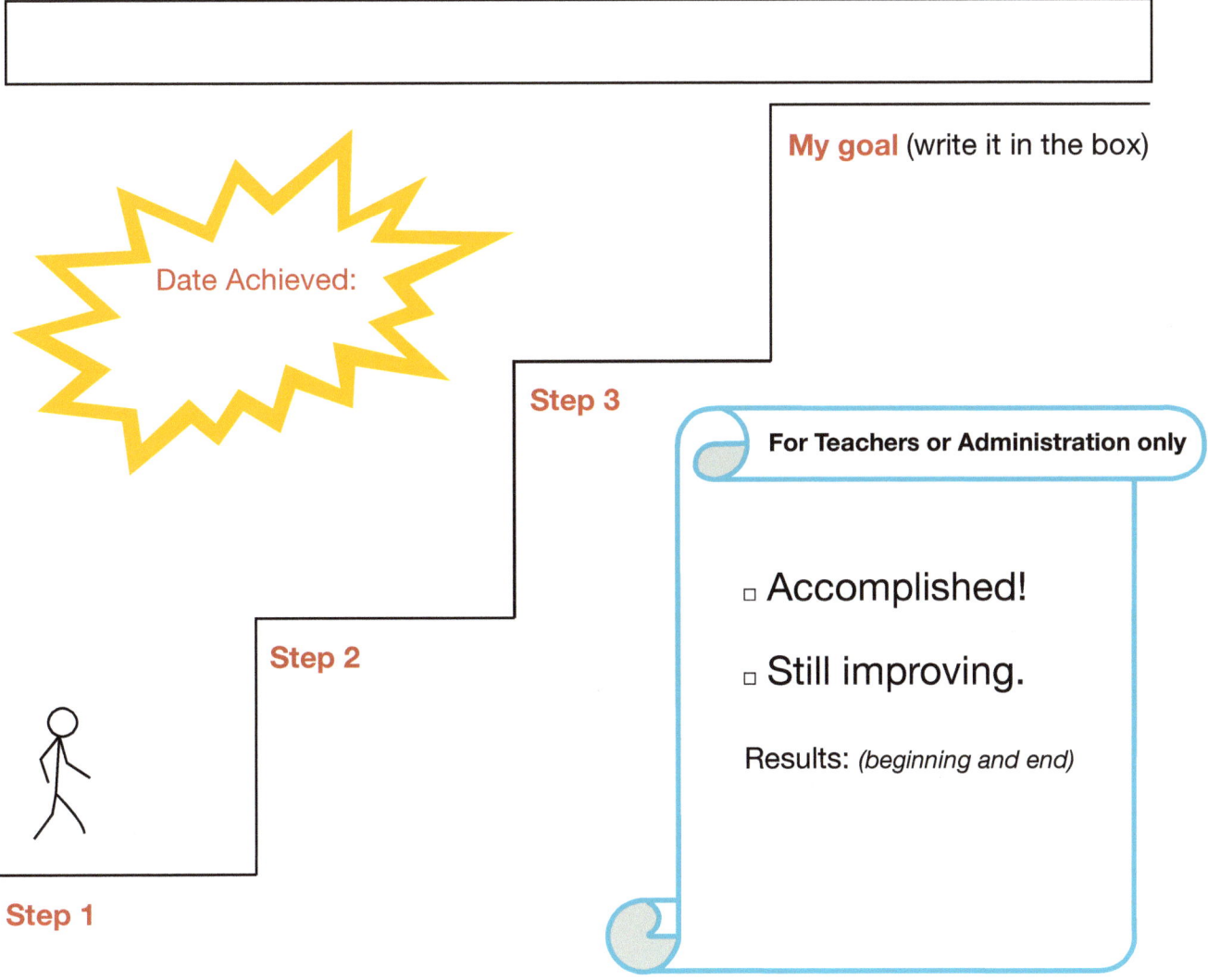

My goal (write it in the box)

Date Achieved:

Step 3

Step 2

Step 1

For Teachers or Administration only

☐ **Accomplished!**

☐ **Still improving.**

Results: *(beginning and end)*

Week 1-8

Students must complete a goal before moving on to the next goal.

Name:

Weekly SMART Goals for

Start Date:

Directions: Circle one of the following: **academic, behavior, attendance.**
Teacher   Counselor   Secretary

SMART goals for success!

S - Specific   Know what you want to achieve!
M - Measurable   How will you know when you reach your goal?
A - Achievable   What steps will you take to reach your goal?
R - Realistic   Set goals you are able to accomplish.
T - Timely   How long will it take to reach your goal?

My goal (write it in the box)

Date Achieved:

Step 3

For Teachers or Administration only

☐ Accomplished!

☐ Still improving.

Results: *(beginning and end)*

Step 2

Step 1

70

College Systems Handout

Take these steps to prepare for acceptance at a University of California (UC)
- Fulfill the A-G requirement by the end of high school
- Graduate and receive your diploma from high school
- Earn as many A's and B's as possible
- Have a minimum 3.0 GPA
- Take the PSAT your sophomore year of high school
- Take the SAT or ACT your junior year, and once again by the end of your senior year (take either or both the SAT/ACT)
- To assist in paying for college, apply for financial aid before the deadline

Take these steps to prepare for acceptance at a California State University (CSU)
- Fulfill the A-G requirement by the end of high school
- Graduate and receive your diploma from high school
- Earn as many A's and B's as possible
- Have a minimum 2.0 GPA
- Take the PSAT your sophomore year of high school
- Take the SAT or ACT your junior year, and once again by the end of your senior year (take either or both the SAT/ACT)
- To assist in paying for college, apply for financial aid before the deadline

Take these steps to prepare for acceptance at a Community College/Junior College (JC)
- Take some A-G courses during high school
- Graduate and receive your diploma from high school
- Earn as many A's and B's as possible
- Contact each college you want to attend to find out its minimum GPA requirement
- Take the PSAT your sophomore year of high school
- Take the SAT or ACT – it will not hurt to have it on your records (take either or both the SAT/ACT)
- To assist in paying for college, apply for financial aid before the deadline

A-G Requirement Handout

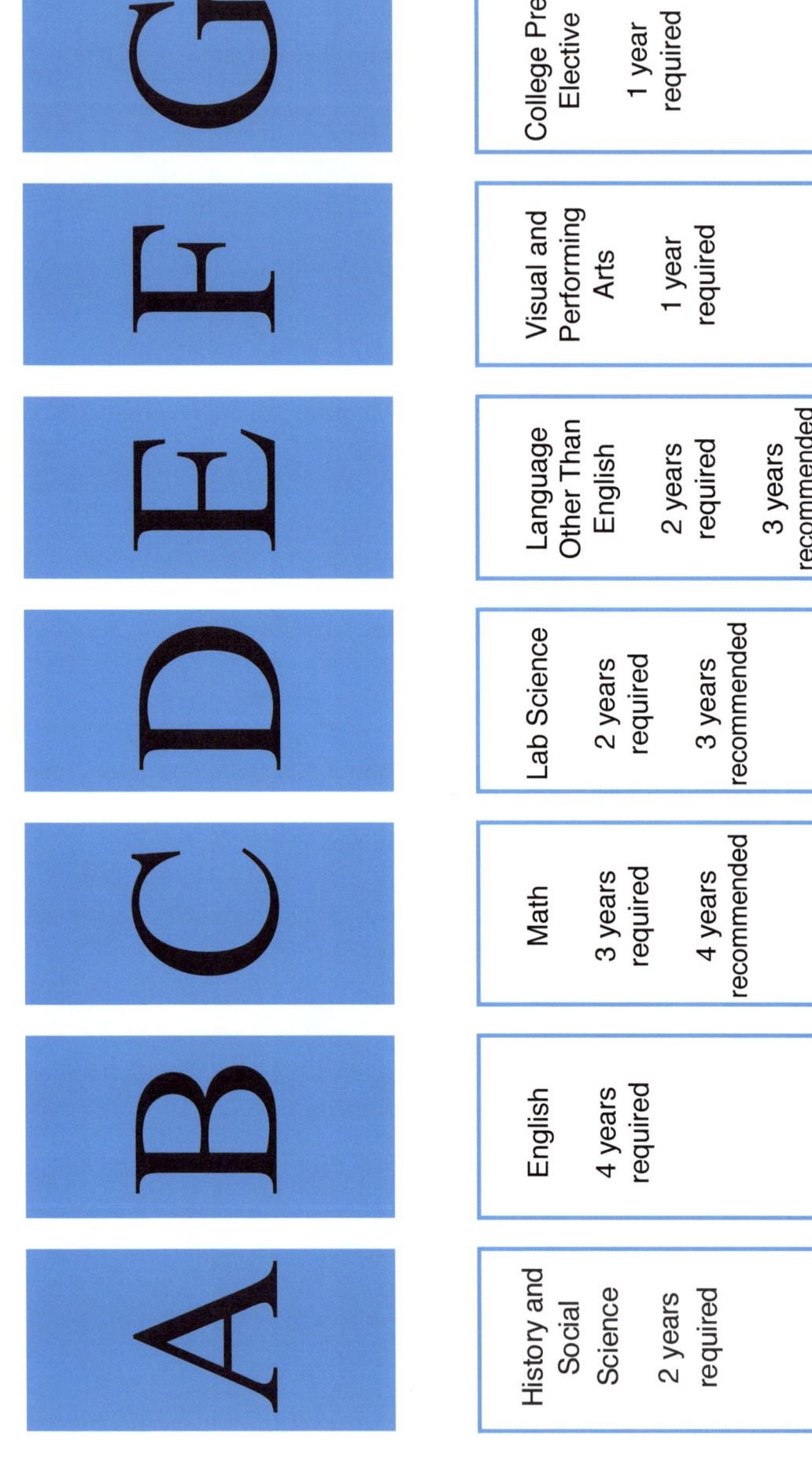

A	B	C	D	E	F	G
History and Social Science 2 years required	English 4 years required	Math 3 years required 4 years recommended	Lab Science 2 years required 3 years recommended	Language Other Than English 2 years required 3 years recommended	Visual and Performing Arts 1 year required	College Prep Elective 1 year required

Path to College Quiz

Answer Key

1. Can you obtain a Ph.D. at a California State University (CSU)?   ■ Yes   ☐ No

2. Do most Community Colleges require you to take the SAT or ACT?   ☐ Yes   ■ No

3. What is the highest level of education a person can obtain?
   - ☐ Associate degree (A.A.)
   - ☐ High school diploma
   - ☐ Master's degree (M.A., M.S.)
   - ■ Doctoral or professional degree (Ph.D., J.D., M.D.)
   - ☐ Bachelor's degree (B.A., B.S.)

4. The following are either part of a 2-year college or 4-year university system. Check the one that *does not* apply:

   - ☐ University of California
   - ☐ California State University
   - ☐ Vocational College
   - ■ Magnet School
   - ☐ Career College

5. The A-G requirements are classes you must take and pass in order to:

   - ☐ Graduate from high school
   - ☐ Get into graduate school
   - ■ Get accepted to a University of California (UC) or California State University (CSU)
   - ☐ Take the SAT or ACT
   - ☐ Gain acceptance into a trade school

Financial Aid & Grants Handout

There are **FOUR** types of financial aid: ***scholarships, grants, loans,*** and ***employment.***

Scholarships: Scholarships are private money given to students from community groups, donors, or the university. The great thing about scholarships is that you do not have to pay them back.

Federal grants: There are four types of federal student aid grants, one specialized grant, and loan combo. All grants are awarded based on the information you submit to FASFA. FASFA bases the grants on financial need by calculating your expected family contribution (EFC).

State grants: These grants are for California state residents only (or your state, if you're outside of California). Your residency status is usually determined by your university's Office of Admission at the time of your application.

Federal loans: These are loans from the federal government. You must pay back the funds given to you.

Private loans: Private lenders give you these loans based on your credit. These loans help bridge the gap between the actual cost of your tuition, your other financial aid funds, and the amount you will contribute.

Employment: This federal work study offers employment opportunities to students and is federally funded. The program usually has limited space. However, if given the opportunity, you can benefit from this program. Work study is also given to students with the highest financial need.

Financial Aid Crossword Puzzle

Answer Key

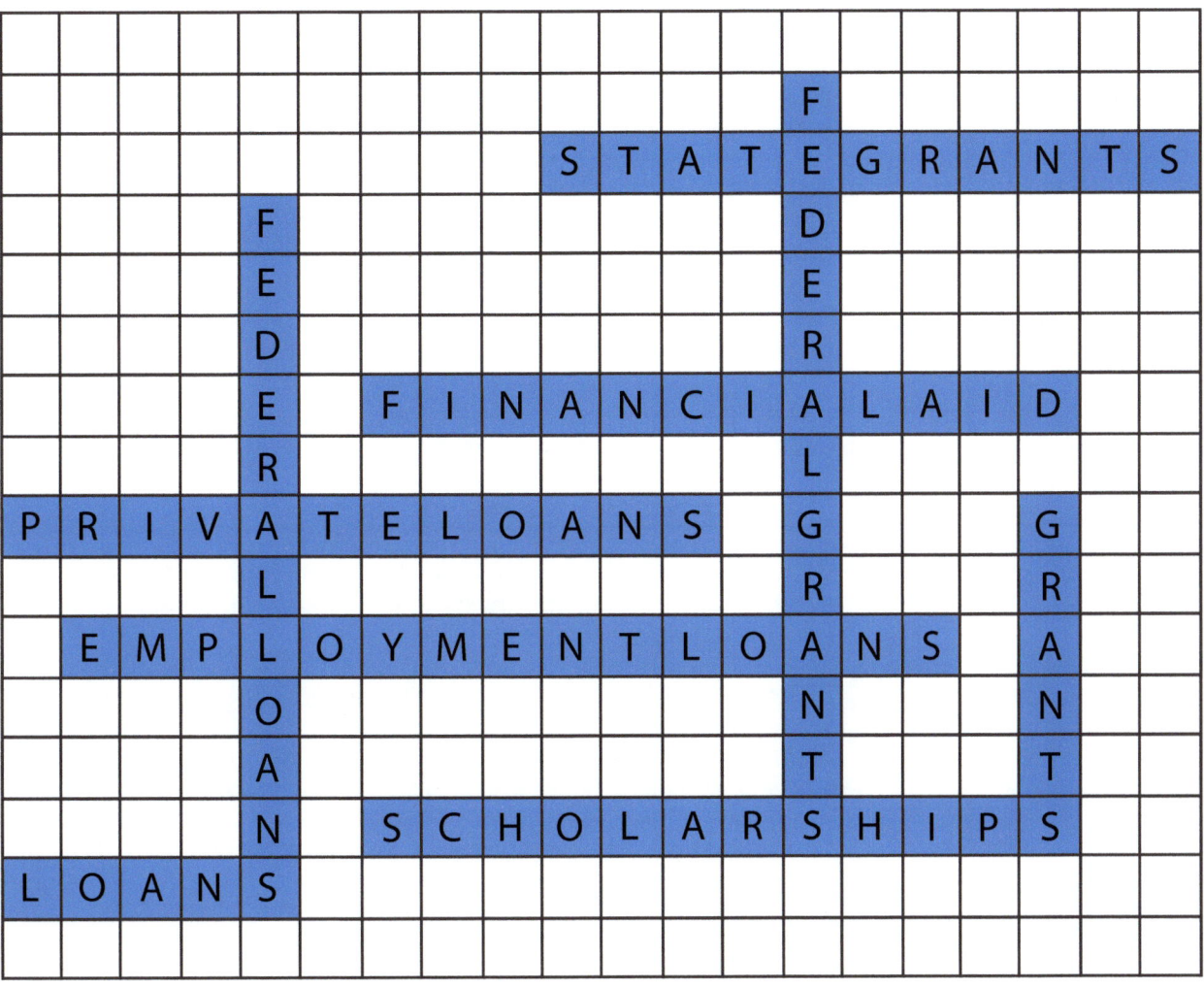

Sample Lesson Plan with Definitions

	SCALE High Lesson Plan
SCALE Standards	Serves as a basis for the SCALE High curriculum and defines the levels for quality of instruction to setting goals in the areas of school, career, and life. The standards also define student learning outcomes.
Anticipatory Set	A statement or activity that should help the student mentally or physically prepare for the lesson. It should always relate to some previous learning.
Objective	A specific result that the student will achieve within a given timeframe, if given access to available resources.
Essential Question	A question asked to stimulate thought, provoke inquiry, and spark more questions during the lesson.
Purpose	The reason behind why the lesson is being taught.
Input	Outlines the steps you should follow to teach the lesson, and refers to the instruction you will provide to help your student understand the lesson's objective and purpose.
Modeling	Refers to the examples that you will provide during the lesson.
Check for Understanding	The process whereby you continually verify that the student is learning what is being taught, while it is being taught.
Guided Practice	The interactive instruction between yourself and your student.
Closure (EQ. Answer)	This is the time when you wrap up a lesson. Help the student organize the information in context, and answer the essential question.
Independent Practice	The part of the lesson where the student is given the opportunity to practice a concept on their own time, and master the skill presented in the lesson.
Materials	The instructional materials or resources used by both yourself and your student.

Tips for Working with Students

Always remember to:
- Set SMART goals with your student.
- Begin where the student is successful.
- Encourage their hard work.
- Speak in a kind and calm manner.
- Listen to what your student says.
- Be patient.

Use positive words like the following to encourage your student:
- That's great!
- How impressive!
- You make it look easy.
- I like the way you are working.
- I am so proud of you.
- That is an interesting way of looking at it.
- Way to go!
- That is a great improvement.
- I like that idea.
- Genius!
- You rock!
- I knew you could do it!

Acknowledgements

SCALE High's goal-setting curriculum is designed for high school students to reflect—examine and interpret—upon their life experiences and transform their deepest passions into reality. This reflection process allows students to become more self-aware and discover how their gifts and talents can be of service to the world.

SCALE High hopes to partner with high schools (public or private); districts; county offices of education; group homes; and other educational institutions, community organizations, and businesses.

Dupé Aleru

Founder and Owner of Tutors for Tots, Tweens & Teens LLC

Acknowledgements

Many thanks to Mr. Saldana—the former Principal at Beach High School in Long Beach, CA—who was the first person to give us the opportunity to implement our program. Also, a special thanks to Abigail Aparicio, who kindly volunteered to help launch the SCALE High Program during the Fall of 2014. Last but not least, thank you to the teachers, who have always been an inspiration to this work.

About the Founder

Dupé Aleru is an entrepreneur, curriculum developer, business coach, and motivational speaker.

As an alumna of California State University, Long Beach, Dupé obtained a B.A. in Sociology and a Multiple Subject Teaching Credential. She also holds a M.S. in Educational Counseling and a Pupil Personnel Services Credential from the University of La Verne.

After four years of teaching for Long Beach Unified School District, Dupé took a job as the Director of Education Services for *The Beverly Hills Courier,* where she built the education section of the newspaper from the ground up, in less than one year.

In 2010, she founded Tutors for Tots, Tweens & Teens LLC—one of Southern California's elite educational companies for students PK-12. Her body of work includes, "The Cook Book" 12-episode web series, its spin-off program "The Cook Book Nutrition Course," the SCALE High Program, and a children's book titled *Animals in Action A-Z.*

Copyright © 2017 by Dupé Aleru and Tutors for Tots, Tweens & Teens LLC. All rights reserved.

Dupé Aleru

Tutors for Tots, Tweens & Teens LLC

5541 E. 7th Street

Long Beach, CA 90804

(562) 856-2801

www.tutorsfortots.com

info@tutorfortots.com

SCALE High Program

www.scalehigh.org

scalehigh@scalehigh.org

www.ingramcontent.com/pod-product-compliance
Lightning Source LLC
Chambersburg PA
CBHW042002150426
43194CB00002B/89